Wallace Bruce, James David Smillie

The Yosemite

Wallace Bruce, James David Smillie

The Yosemite

ISBN/EAN: 9783744661492

Printed in Europe, USA, Canada, Australia, Japan

Cover: Foto ©Andreas Hilbeck / pixelio.de

More available books at **www.hansebooks.com**

THE

YOSEMITE.

BY

WALLACE BRUCE.

ILLUSTRATED BY

JAMES D. SMILLIE.

PUBLISHED BY
LEE AND SHEPARD,
BOSTON, MASS.
CHARLES T. DILLINGHAM,
NEW YORK.
1880.

S. W. GREEN'S SON,
Printer,
NEW YORK.

PHOTO-ENGRAVING CO.
(Moss Process),
NEW YORK.

List of Illustrations,

BY

JAS. D. SMILLIE.

FRONTISPIECE—"To Annie."

STANZA VII.

"Glacier Rock from Tenaya Cañon."

STANZA VIII.

"South Dome and Cloud's Rest."

STANZA IX.

"Mirror Lake and Tenaya Cañon."

STANZA X.

"Glacier Rock, Vernal Point, and Mt. Starr King."

STANZA XI.

"Nevada and Vernal Falls and the High Sierras."

STANZA XII.

"Po-ho-no, or Bridal Veil Fall."

STANZA XIII.

"The Cap of Liberty and Nevada Fall."

STANZA XIV.

"Yosemite Valley from Cloud's Rest."

FINIS.

"Yosemite Fall and Merced River."

THE YOSEMITE.

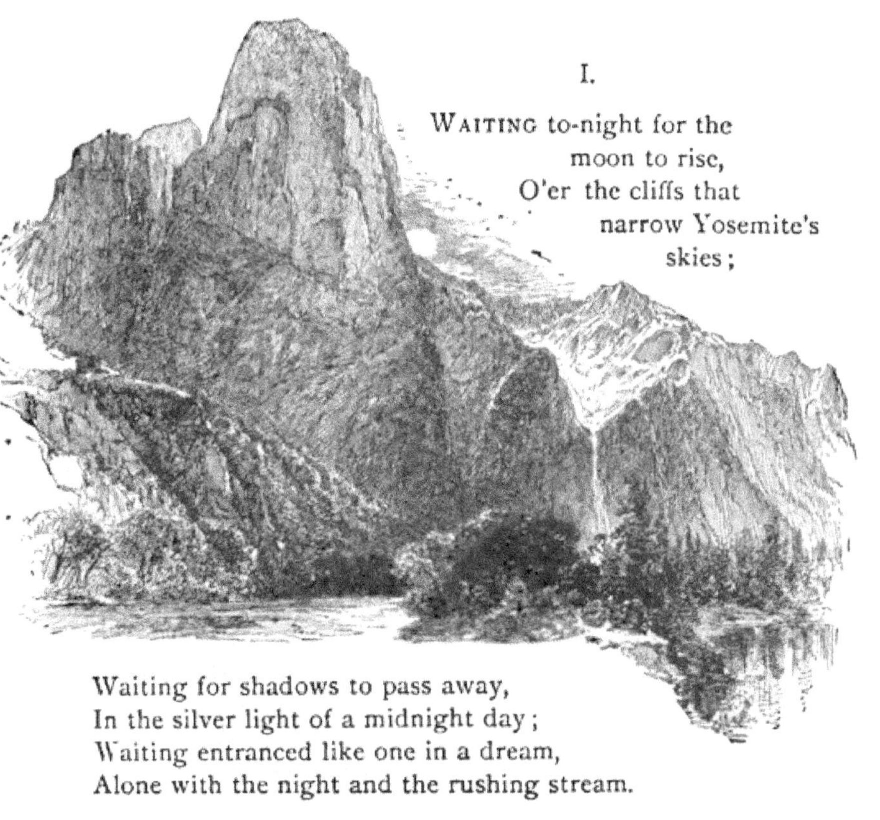

I.

WAITING to-night for the
moon to rise,
O'er the cliffs that
narrow Yosemite's
skies;

Waiting for shadows to pass away,
In the silver light of a midnight day;
Waiting entranced like one in a dream,
Alone with the night and the rushing stream.

II.

Alone in a Temple vast and grand,
With spire and turret on every hand—
A world's Cathedral with walls sublime
Chiselled and carved by the hand of time,

And over all
a starlit dome,
Beneath whose arch we dream of home.

III.

But the darkling shadows dissolve, and now
The moonlight touches "El Capitan's" brow,

And the lesser stars grow pale and dim
Along the sheer-cut mountain rim;
And, touched with magic, the gray walls stand
The living dream of a fairy land.

IV.

Yet I know it is real,
for I see the spray
Of Yosemite Fall in
the moonlight play,
Swaying and trembling—
a radiant glow,
From the sky above
to the vale below;
Like the ladder of old
to Jacob given,
A line of light from
earth to heaven.

V.

And there comes to my soul
a vision dear
Of angel forms
and voices here;
And I feel the sweet and
wondrous power
Of a Presence that fills
the midnight hour;
And I know that Bethel
is everywhere—
For prayer is the foot
of the angel stair.

VI.

A light divine—a holy rest—
Floods all the valley
and fills my breast;
The very mountains are
hushed in sleep,

From Eagle Point
to Sentinel Peak;
And a life-long lesson is
taught me to-night,
When shrouded in shadow
to wait for the light.

VII.

Waiting at dawn for the morn to break,
By the crystal waters of Mirror Lake;
Waiting to see the mountains gray,
Clearly defined in the light of day;
Reflected and throned in beauty here—
A lakelet that seems but "The Valley's Tear."

VIII.

Waiting—but look! for the Dome so bright
Is floating now in a sea of light;
And Cloud's Rest, glistening
with caps of snow,
Inverted stands in
the vale below,

With tow'ring peaks
and cliffs on high
Hanging to meet another sky.

IX.

O crystal gem in setting rare!

O soul-like mirror
in middle air!
O forest-heart of
eternal love—
Earth-born, but pure
as heaven above!
This Sabbath morn
we find in thee
The poet's dream of purity.

X.

The hours pass by, and I'm waiting now
On Glacier Point's o'erhanging brow,
Waiting to see the picture pass,
Like the fleeting show
of a magic glass—
Waiting—and still
the vision seems
Woven of light and
colored with dreams.

XI.

But the cloud-capped towers,
and pillars gray,
Securely stand in
the light of day;
The Temple wall is
firm and sure;
The worshippers pass,
but It shall endure—
And will while loud
Yosemite calls
To bright Nevada and Vernal Falls.

XII.

O grand and majestic organ-choir
With deep-toned voices that never tire!
O anthem written in notes that glow
On the rainbow bars of Po-ho-no!

O sweet "Te Deum" forever sung
With spray of incense heavenward swung!

XIII.

Thy music my soul with rapture thrills,
And there comes to my lips,
"The templed hills,
Thy rocks and rills"
—a nation's song,
From valley to mountain
borne along;

My country's temple, built for thee,
Crowned with the "Cap of Liberty"!

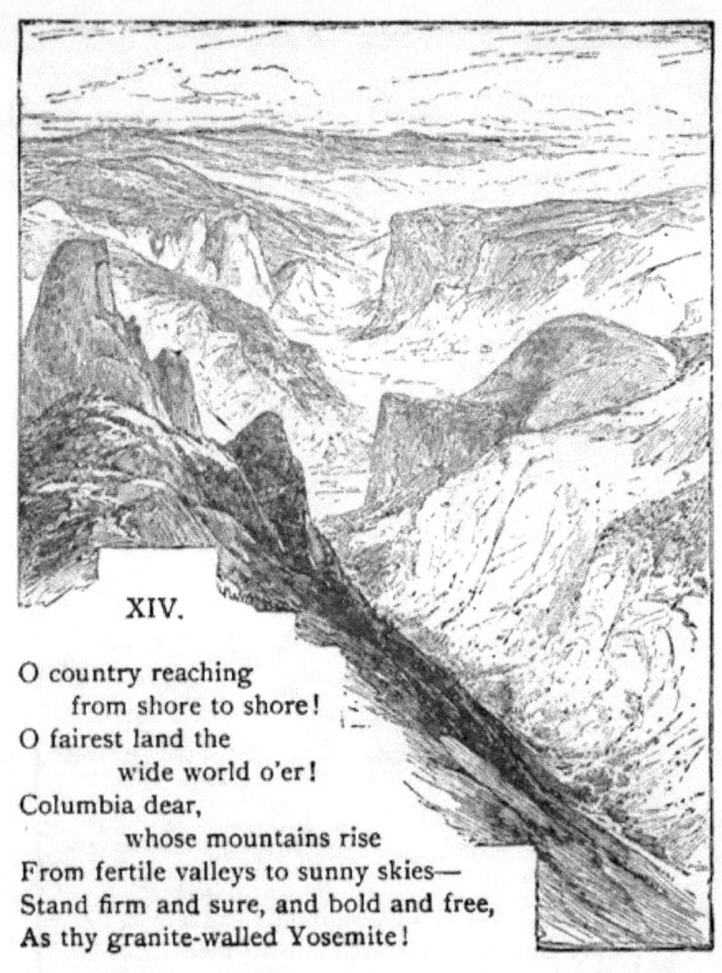

XIV.

O country reaching
from shore to shore!
O fairest land the
wide world o'er!
Columbia dear,
whose mountains rise
From fertile valleys to sunny skies—
Stand firm and sure, and bold and free,
As thy granite-walled Yosemite!

YOSEMITE FALL AND MERCED RIVER.

www.ingramcontent.com/pod-product-compliance
Lightning Source LLC
Chambersburg PA
CBHW021612270326
41931CB00009B/1447
* 9 7 8 3 7 4 4 6 6 1 4 9 2 *